Teach Your Child to Read

300 Short Easy Sentences

English - Hindi

Name

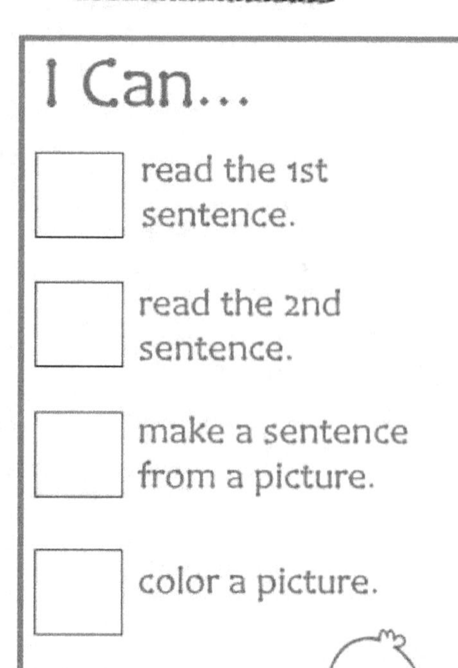

The frog is going to a party.

मेंढक एक पार्टी में जा रहा है।

The happy frog is wearing a green hat.

आनंदी मेंढक हरे रंग की टोपी पहने हुए है।

Name 

I Can...

- [ ] read the 1st sentence.
- [ ] read the 2nd sentence.
- [ ] make a sentence from a picture.
- [ ] color a picture.
- [ ] Draw a picture.

Owl likes to read big books.

उल्लू को बड़ी किताबें पढ़ना पसंद है।

A smart owl is reading an alphabet book.

एक स्मार्ट उल्लू एक वर्णमाला पुस्तक पढ़ रहा है।

Name

I Can...

- [ ] read the 1st sentence.
- [ ] read the 2nd sentence.
- [ ] make a sentence from a picture.
- [ ] color a picture.
- [ ] Draw a picture.

Come on! The ice cream truck is here!

आओ! आइसक्रीम ट्रक यहाँ है!

He is driving a big icecream truck.

वह एक बड़ा प्रतिष्ठित ट्रक चला रहा है।

Name

I Can...

- [ ] read the 1st sentence.
- [ ] read the 2nd sentence.
- [ ] make a sentence from a picture.
- [ ] color a picture.
- [ ] Draw a picture.

Dragons are very friendly and have scales on their backs.

ड्रेगन बहुत अनुकूल हैं और उनकी पीठ पर तराजू हैं।

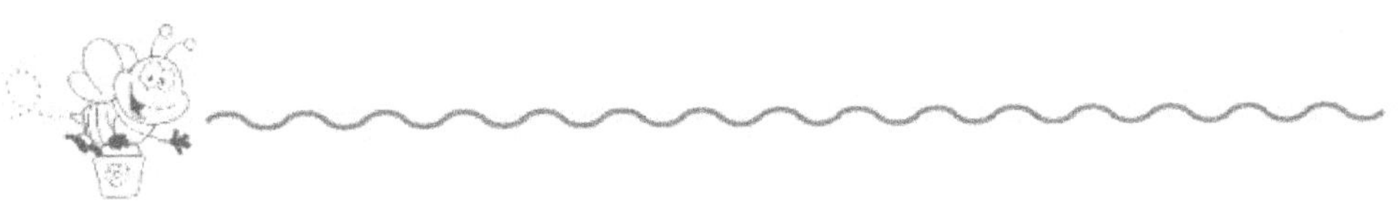

The dragon is waving his hand.

अजगर अपना हाथ लहरा रहा है।

Name

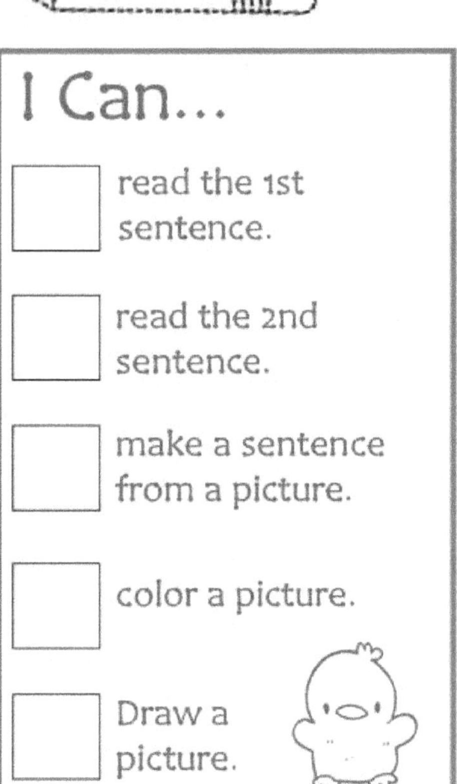

This ram lives in the farmhouse.

यह राम फार्महाउस में रहता है।

Ram has a large horn and fluffy wool.

राम के पास एक बड़ा सींग और शराबी ऊन है।

Name

I Can...

- [ ] read the 1st sentence.
- [ ] read the 2nd sentence.
- [ ] make a sentence from a picture.
- [ ] color a picture.
- [ ] Draw a picture.

The bunny likes to eat carrots.

बन्नी को गाजर खाना पसंद है।

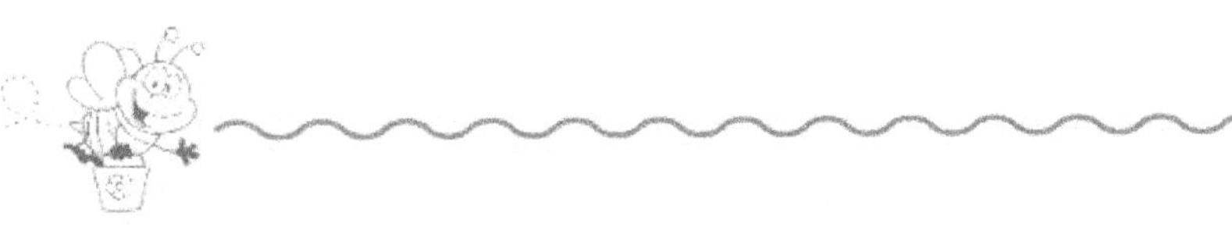

Rabbit thinks that the juicy orange carrot looks yummy.

खरगोश सोचता है कि रसदार नारंगी गाजर स्वादिष्ट लगता है।

Name

I Can...

- [ ] read the 1st sentence.
- [ ] read the 2nd sentence.
- [ ] make a sentence from a picture.
- [ ] color a picture.
- [ ] Draw a picture.

The clown likes to give out balloons to little kids.

विदूषक छोटे बच्चों को गुब्बारे देना पसंद करता है।

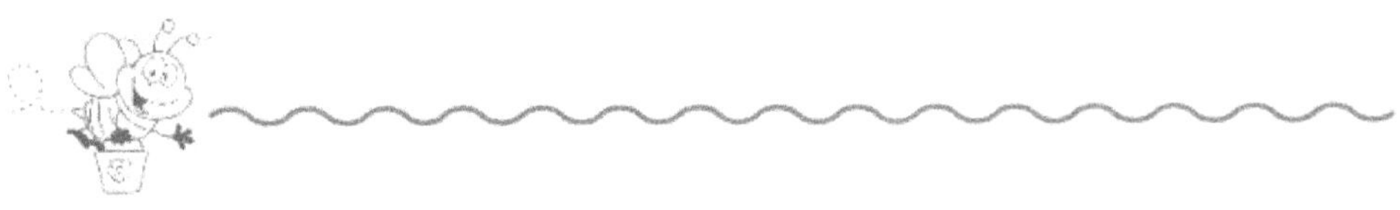

Funny, Mr. Clown is giving away colorful balloons.

मजेदार, मिस्टर क्लाउन दूर रंगीन गुब्बारे दे रहा है।

Name

I Can...

- [ ] read the 1st sentence.
- [ ] read the 2nd sentence.
- [ ] make a sentence from a picture.
- [ ] color a picture.
- [ ] Draw a picture.

The clown is juggling balls for his performance.

मसखरा अपने प्रदर्शन के लिए गेंदों की बाजीगरी कर रहा है।

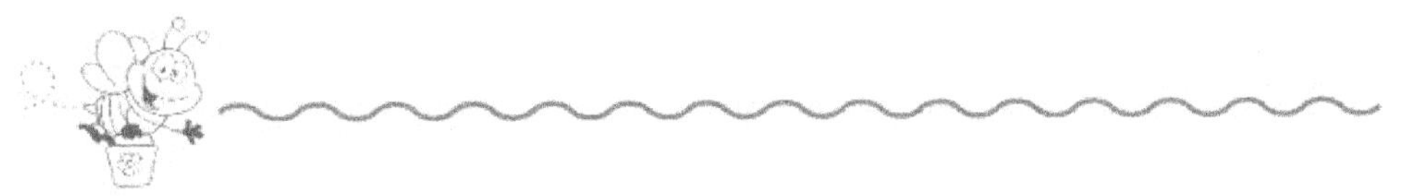

Talented, Mr. Clown is juggling five red balls.

प्रतिभाशाली, मिस्टर क्लाउन पांच लाल गेंदों की बाजीगरी कर रहे हैं।

Name

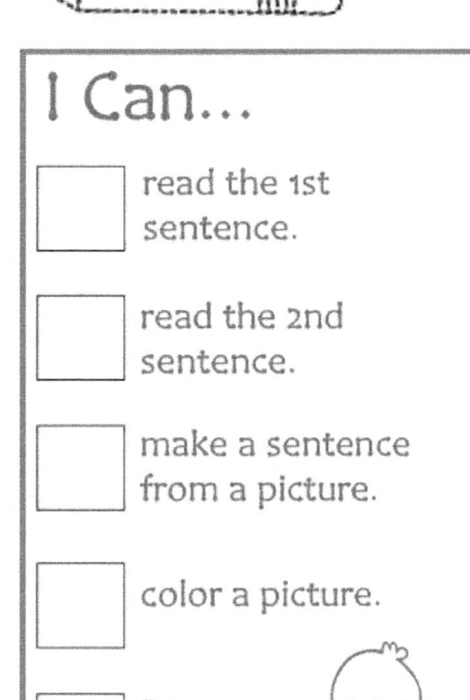

The Easter Bunny is going to give out chocolate eggs.

ईस्टर बनी चॉकलेट अंडे देने जा रही है।

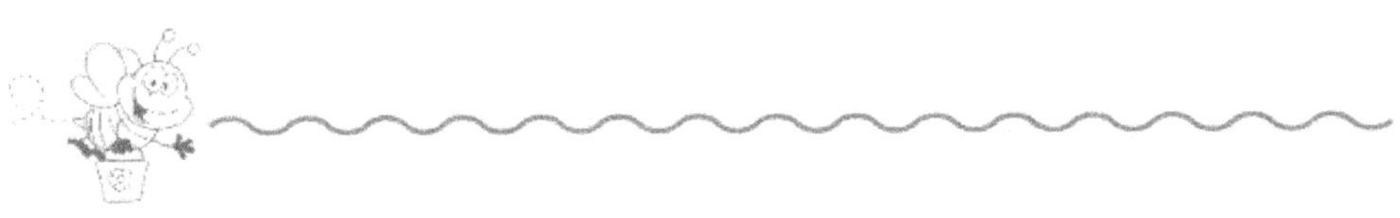

The rabbit goes out to buy more orange carrots.

अधिक नारंगी गाजर खरीदने के लिए खरगोश बाहर जाता है।

Name

I Can...

- [ ] read the 1st sentence.
- [ ] read the 2nd sentence.
- [ ] make a sentence from a picture.
- [ ] color a picture.
- [ ] Draw a picture.

The pencil is drawing a zig-zag line.

पेंसिल एक ज़िग-ज़ैग रेखा खींच रहा है।

The Pencil is saying hello to you.

पेंसिल तुम्हें नमस्ते कह रही है।

Name

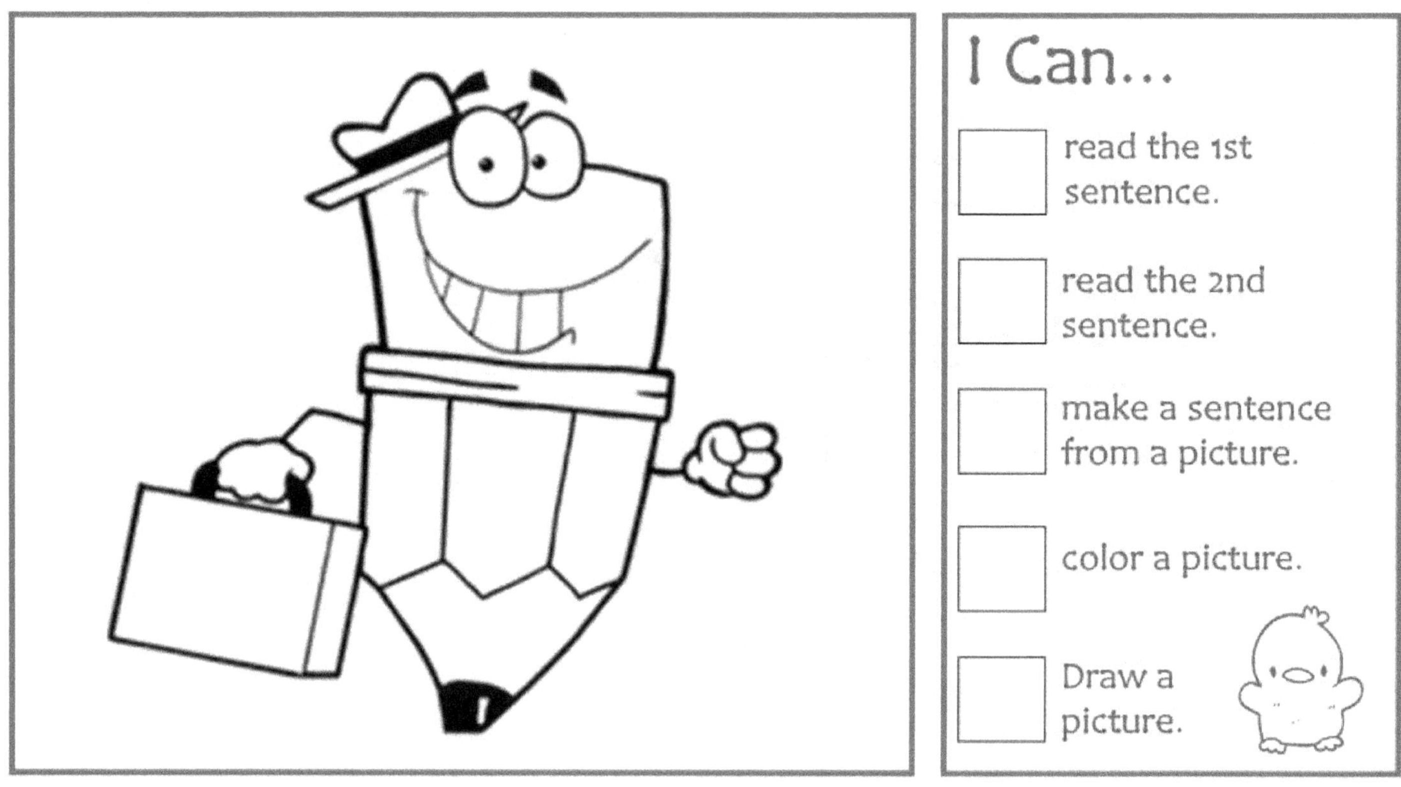

The pencil put on a big smile and went to work.

पेंसिल ने एक बड़ी सी मुस्कान डाली और काम पर चली गई।

The Pencil is leaving to go on a long relaxing vacation.

पेंसिल लंबी आराम की छुट्टी पर जाने के लिए छोड़ रही है।

Name

I Can...

- read the 1st sentence.
- read the 2nd sentence.
- make a sentence from a picture.
- color a picture.
- Draw a picture.

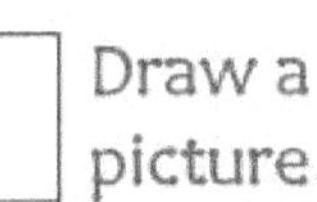

This snowman is my friend, and he is a helper of Santa.

यह हिममानव मेरा दोस्त है, और वह सांता का सहायक है।

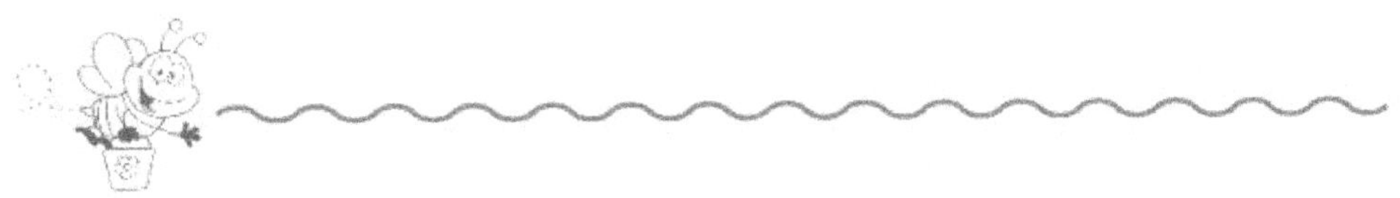

Mr. Snowman is celebrating Christmas by the decorated tree.

श्री स्नोमैन सजाए गए पेड़ द्वारा क्रिसमस मना रहे हैं।

Name

I Can...

- read the 1st sentence.
- read the 2nd sentence.
- make a sentence from a picture.
- color a picture.
- Draw a picture.

The octopus is working as a chef and serving food.

ऑक्टोपस एक शेफ के रूप में काम कर रहा है और भोजन परोस रहा है।

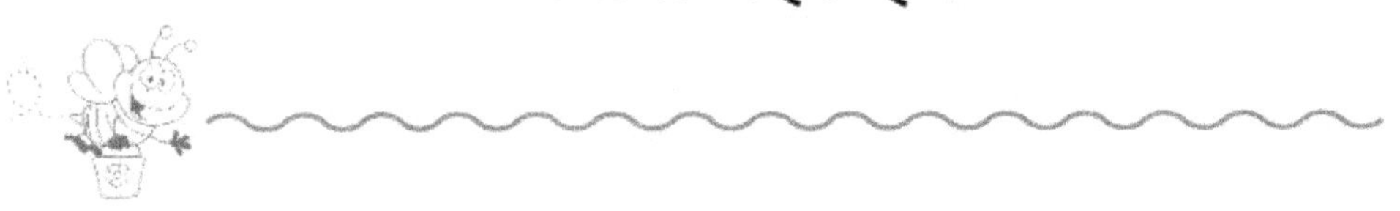

Chef Octopus is serving a delicious turkey dinner.

शेफ ऑक्टोपस एक स्वादिष्ट टर्की रात का खाना परोस रहा है।

Name

I Can...

- read the 1st sentence.
- read the 2nd sentence.
- make a sentence from a picture.
- color a picture.
- Draw a picture.

Santa is happy.

संता खुश है।

Santa Claus is giving extraordinary presents to excited kids.

सांता क्लॉज उत्साहित बच्चों को असाधारण उपहार दे रहा है।

Name

I Can...

- [ ] read the 1st sentence.
- [ ] read the 2nd sentence.
- [ ] make a sentence from a picture.
- [ ] color a picture.
- [ ] Draw a picture.

The bear likes to eat sweets.

भालू को मिठाई खाना पसंद है।

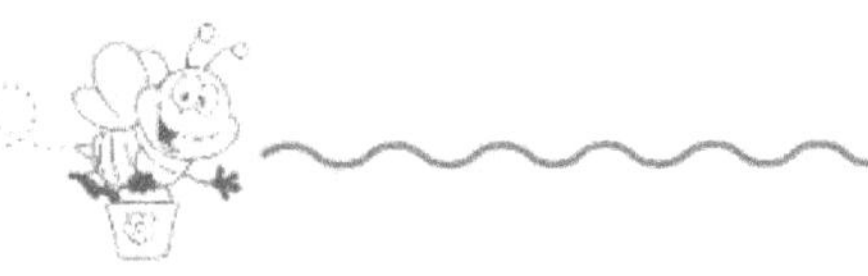

Teddy is licking a red and white candy cane.

टेडी एक लाल और सफेद कैंडी बेंत चाट रहा है।

Name

I Can...

- [ ] read the 1st sentence.
- [ ] read the 2nd sentence.
- [ ] make a sentence from a picture.
- [ ] color a picture.
- [ ] Draw a picture.

The book has a wand.

पुस्तक में एक छड़ी है।

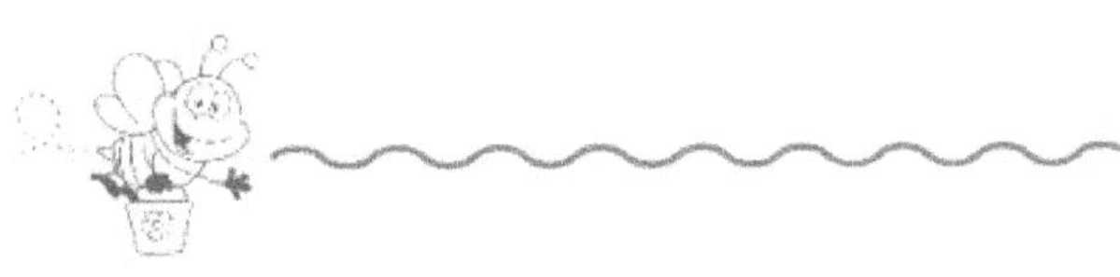

The cereal box got a magician set for Christmas.

अनाज के बक्से को क्रिसमस के लिए एक जादूगर सेट मिला।

Name

I Can...

- [ ] read the 1st sentence.
- [ ] read the 2nd sentence.
- [ ] make a sentence from a picture.
- [ ] color a picture.
- [ ] Draw a picture.

The bear has a present.

भालू का एक वर्तमान है।

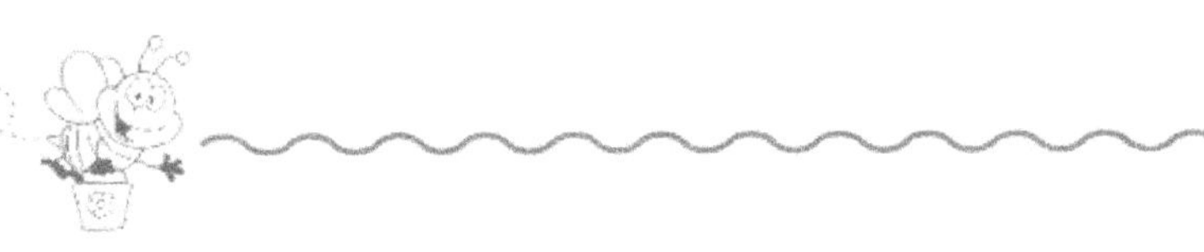

Happy Teddy is opening his box of presents from Santa.

हैप्पी टेडी सांता से उपहारों का पिटारा खोल रहा है।

Name

I Can...

- read the 1st sentence.
- read the 2nd sentence.
- make a sentence from a picture.
- color a picture.
- Draw a picture.

Santa is going to give out presents.

सांता प्रस्तुत करने जा रहा है।

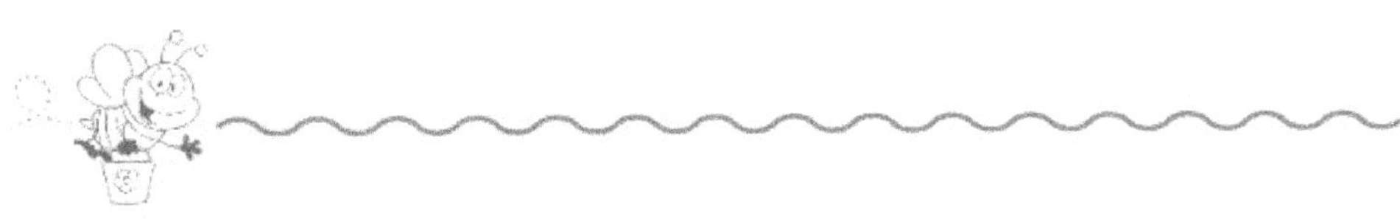

Santa is lugging a large brown bag of gifts to his sley.

सांता अपनी गली में उपहारों का एक बड़ा भूरा बैग लुटा रहा है।

Name

I Can...

- [ ] read the 1st sentence.
- [ ] read the 2nd sentence.
- [ ] make a sentence from a picture.
- [ ] color a picture.
- [ ] Draw a picture.

I made a snowman.

मैंने एक स्नोमैन बनाया।

Mr. Snowman is holding a broom and saying goodbye.

श्री स्नोमैन एक झाड़ू पकड़कर अलविदा कह रहे हैं।

Name

I Can...

- [ ] read the 1st sentence.
- [ ] read the 2nd sentence.
- [ ] make a sentence from a picture.
- [ ] color a picture.
- [ ] Draw a picture.

The parrot is colorful.

तोता रंगीन है।

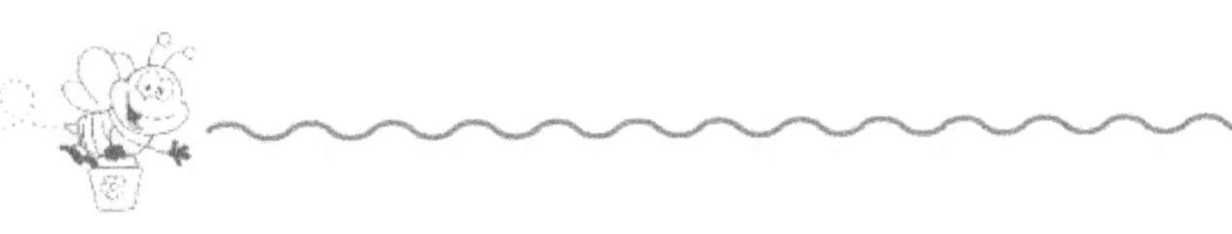

The green parrot came from the forest to the zoo.

हरे तोते जंगल से चिड़ियाघर आए थे।

Name

I Can...

- [ ] read the 1st sentence.
- [ ] read the 2nd sentence.
- [ ] make a sentence from a picture.
- [ ] color a picture.
- [ ] Draw a picture.

There are a lot of animals.

बहुत सारे जानवर हैं।

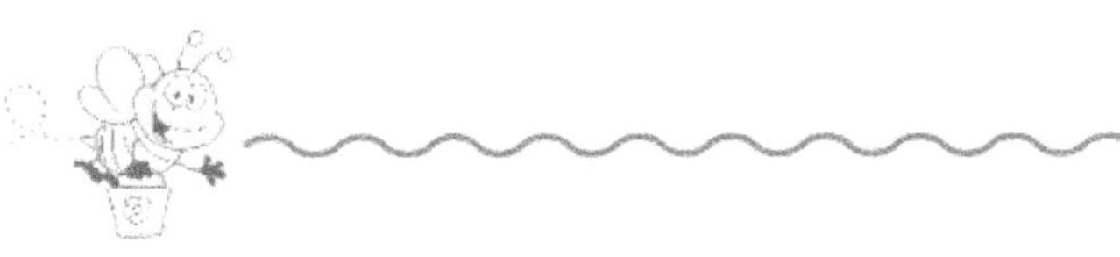

The animals are happy being together again.

जानवर फिर से एक साथ होने से खुश हैं।

Name

I Can...

- [ ] read the 1st sentence.
- [ ] read the 2nd sentence.
- [ ] make a sentence from a picture.
- [ ] color a picture.
- [ ] Draw a picture.

The man is wearing a belt.

आदमी ने बेल्ट पहन रखी है।

The carpenter is fixing something.

बढ़ई कुछ ठीक कर रहा है।

Name

I Can...

- [ ] read the 1st sentence.
- [ ] read the 2nd sentence.
- [ ] make a sentence from a picture.
- [ ] color a picture.
- [ ] Draw a picture.

The rabbit is very young.

खरगोश बहुत छोटा है।

The magician plays a trick.

जादूगर एक चाल खेलता है।

Name

I Can...

- [ ] read the 1st sentence.
- [ ] read the 2nd sentence.
- [ ] make a sentence from a picture.
- [ ] color a picture.
- [ ] Draw a picture.

He has a potion.

उसके पास एक औषधि है।

The scientist is making a potion.

वैज्ञानिक एक औषधि बना रहा है।

Name

I Can...

- read the 1st sentence.
- read the 2nd sentence.
- make a sentence from a picture.
- color a picture.
- Draw a picture.

He is wearing sunglasses.

उसने धूप का चश्मा पहन रखा है।

The policeman is mad.

पुलिस वाला पागल है।

Name

I Can...

- read the 1st sentence.
- read the 2nd sentence.
- make a sentence from a picture.
- color a picture.
- Draw a picture.

He has a bucket of paint.

उसके पास पेंट की बाल्टी है।

He likes to paint.

उसे पेंट करना पसंद है।

Name

I Can...

- read the 1st sentence.
- read the 2nd sentence.
- make a sentence from a picture.
- color a picture.
- Draw a picture.

The man has a hat.

आदमी के पास टोपी है।

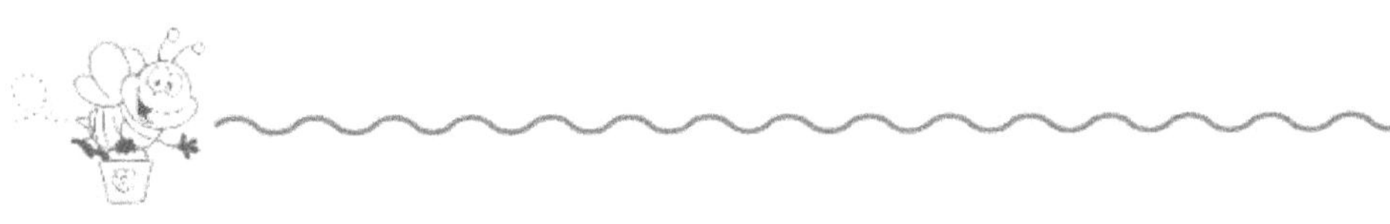

The postman is giving out the mail in the early morning.

डाकिया सुबह-सुबह डाक दे रहा है।

Name

I Can...

- [ ] read the 1st sentence.
- [ ] read the 2nd sentence.
- [ ] make a sentence from a picture.
- [ ] color a picture.
- [ ] Draw a picture.

He has a walkie talkie.

उसके पास वॉकी टॉकी है।

He is going to work with his suitcase.

वह अपने सूटकेस के साथ काम करने जा रहा है।

Name ______________________

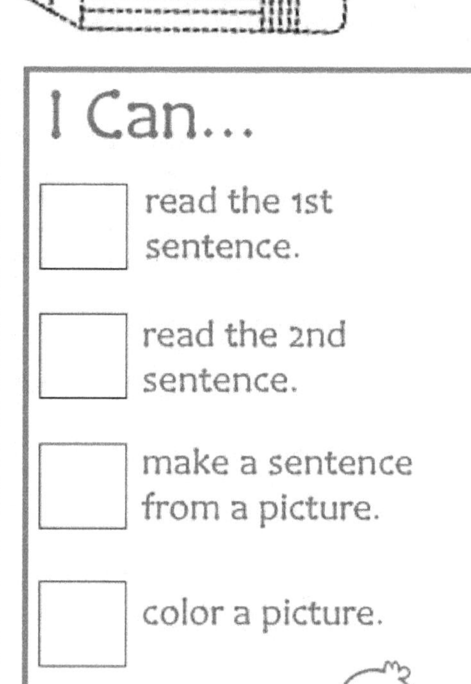

He is sleepy.

उसे नींद आ रही है।

The delivery man sent us a package.

डिलीवरी मैन ने हमें एक पैकेज भेजा।

Name

I Can...

- read the 1st sentence.
- read the 2nd sentence.
- make a sentence from a picture.
- color a picture.
- Draw a picture.

He is wearing a bowtie.

उन्होंने एक धनुष धारण किया हुआ है।

The waiter is serving juice.

वेटर जूस परोस रहा है।

Name

I Can...

- [ ] read the 1st sentence.
- [ ] read the 2nd sentence.
- [ ] make a sentence from a picture.
- [ ] color a picture.
- [ ] Draw a picture.

He has a suitcase.

उसके पास एक सूटकेस है।

The engineer is holding a wrench.

इंजीनियर एक रिंच पकड़ रहा है।

Name

I Can...

- [ ] read the 1st sentence.
- [ ] read the 2nd sentence.
- [ ] make a sentence from a picture.
- [ ] color a picture.
- [ ] Draw a picture.

The chef has a napkin.

महाराज के पास एक नैपकिन है।

The chef serves delicious-looking food.

शेफ स्वादिष्ट दिखने वाला भोजन परोसता है।

Name

I Can...

- read the 1st sentence.
- read the 2nd sentence.
- make a sentence from a picture.
- color a picture.
- Draw a picture.

The rooster has a big beak.

मुर्गे की बड़ी चोंच होती है।

The chicken is saying hello to us.

मुर्गी हमें नमस्ते कह रही है।

Name

I Can...

- [ ] read the 1st sentence.
- [ ] read the 2nd sentence.
- [ ] make a sentence from a picture.
- [ ] color a picture.
- [ ] Draw a picture.

The bird is small.

पक्षी छोटा है।

The chick is on the telephone talking with his friend.

चिक अपने दोस्त के साथ बात कर रहे टेलीफोन पर है।

Name

I Can...

- [ ] read the 1st sentence.
- [ ] read the 2nd sentence.
- [ ] make a sentence from a picture.
- [ ] color a picture.
- [ ] Draw a picture.

That is my ring.

वह मेरी अंगूठी है।

That is a beautiful ring.

वह एक सुंदर वलय है।

Name

I Can...

- [ ] read the 1st sentence.
- [ ] read the 2nd sentence.
- [ ] make a sentence from a picture.
- [ ] color a picture.
- [ ] Draw a picture.

The duck has three eggs.

बत्तख के तीन अंडे होते हैं।

The duck has a big nose.

बत्तख की बड़ी नाक होती है।

Name

I Can...

- [ ] read the 1st sentence.
- [ ] read the 2nd sentence.
- [ ] make a sentence from a picture.
- [ ] color a picture.
- [ ] Draw a picture.

The swan is beautiful.

हंस सुंदर है।

The graceful swan is striding through the water.

सुशोभित हंस पानी के माध्यम से चल रहा है।

Name

I Can...

- [ ] read the 1st sentence.
- [ ] read the 2nd sentence.
- [ ] make a sentence from a picture.
- [ ] color a picture.
- [ ] Draw a picture.

The girl is wearing a dress.

लड़की ने एक ड्रेस पहनी हुई है।

The maid is cleaning our room.

नौकरानी हमारे कमरे की सफाई कर रही है।

Name

I Can...

- read the 1st sentence.
- read the 2nd sentence.
- make a sentence from a picture.
- color a picture.
- Draw a picture.

The boy is running.

लड़का भाग रहा है।

The little boy was running.

छोटा लड़का दौड़ रहा था।

Name

I Can...

- read the 1st sentence.
- read the 2nd sentence.
- make a sentence from a picture.
- color a picture.
- Draw a picture.

He is a musician.

वह एक संगीतकार है।

He is playing a lively tune on his flute.

वह अपनी बांसुरी पर जीवंत धुन बजा रहा है।

Name

I Can...

- read the 1st sentence.
- read the 2nd sentence.
- make a sentence from a picture.
- color a picture.
- Draw a picture.

He looks joyful.

वह हर्षित दिखता है।

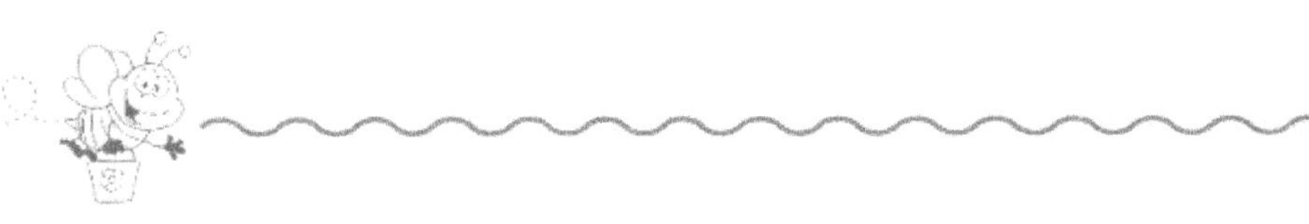

That boy works in a band and plays the drum.

वह लड़का एक बैंड में काम करता है और ड्रम बजाता है।

Name

I Can...

- [ ] read the 1st sentence.
- [ ] read the 2nd sentence.
- [ ] make a sentence from a picture.
- [ ] color a picture.
- [ ] Draw a picture.

The dinosaur is a rock star.

डायनासोर एक रॉक स्टार है।

The dragon is playing the guitar.

ड्रैगन गिटार बजा रहा है।

Name

I Can...

- [ ] read the 1st sentence.
- [ ] read the 2nd sentence.
- [ ] make a sentence from a picture.
- [ ] color a picture.
- [ ] Draw a picture.

The nurse helps the doctor.

नर्स डॉक्टर की मदद करती है।

The nurse looks scary, holding a syringe.

नर्स डरावनी लग रही है, सिरिंज पकड़े हुए।

Name

I Can...

- [ ] read the 1st sentence.
- [ ] read the 2nd sentence.
- [ ] make a sentence from a picture.
- [ ] color a picture.
- [ ] Draw a picture.

She is wearing a crown.

उसने मुकुट पहना हुआ है।

The queen bee has a beautiful wand.

रानी मधुमक्खी के पास एक सुंदर छड़ी है।

Name

I Can...

- read the 1st sentence.
- read the 2nd sentence.
- make a sentence from a picture.
- color a picture.
- Draw a picture.

It is orange and black.

यह नारंगी और काला है।

The tiger is wearing a bow on its neck.

बाघ ने अपनी गर्दन पर धनुष पहना हुआ है।

Name

I Can...

- [ ] read the 1st sentence.
- [ ] read the 2nd sentence.
- [ ] make a sentence from a picture.
- [ ] color a picture.
- [ ] Draw a picture.

The boy is carrying a lot of books.

लड़का बहुत सारी किताबें लेकर जा रहा है।

The boy is carrying so many books!

लड़का इतनी किताबें लेकर जा रहा है!

Name

I Can...

- [ ] read the 1st sentence.
- [ ] read the 2nd sentence.
- [ ] make a sentence from a picture.
- [ ] color a picture.
- [ ] Draw a picture.

The pizza looks delicious.

पिज्जा स्वादिष्ट लगता है।

The waiter is serving steaming hot pizza.

वेटर स्टीमिंग हॉट पिज़्ज़ा परोस रहा है।

Name

I Can...

- [ ] read the 1st sentence.
- [ ] read the 2nd sentence.
- [ ] make a sentence from a picture.
- [ ] color a picture.
- [ ] Draw a picture.

That is my dad's computer.

वह मेरे पिताजी का कंप्यूटर है।

My dad works on the computer.

मेरे पिताजी कंप्यूटर पर काम करते हैं।

Name

I Can...

- read the 1st sentence.
- read the 2nd sentence.
- make a sentence from a picture.
- color a picture.
- Draw a picture.

The farmer has a beard.

किसान की दाढ़ी है।

The gardener is going to plant flowers

माली फूल लगाने जा रहा है

Name

I Can...

- read the 1st sentence.
- read the 2nd sentence.
- make a sentence from a picture.
- color a picture.
- Draw a picture.

The strawberry is red.

स्ट्रॉबेरी लाल है।

I love to drink strawberry juice.

मुझे स्ट्रॉबेरी का रस पीना बहुत पसंद है।

Name

I Can...

- read the 1st sentence.
- read the 2nd sentence.
- make a sentence from a picture.
- color a picture.
- Draw a picture.

The magician has a wand.

जादूगर के पास एक छड़ी है।

The wizard likes to work with magic.

जादूगर जादू के साथ काम करना पसंद करता है।

Name

I Can...

- [ ] read the 1st sentence.
- [ ] read the 2nd sentence.
- [ ] make a sentence from a picture.
- [ ] color a picture.
- [ ] Draw a picture.

Reindeer has a scarf.

बारहसिंगा का दुपट्टा है।

Santa gave reindeer a big present.

संता ने बारहसिंगे को एक बड़ा सा उपहार दिया।

Name

I Can...

- [ ] read the 1st sentence.
- [ ] read the 2nd sentence.
- [ ] make a sentence from a picture.
- [ ] color a picture.
- [ ] Draw a picture.

I have a lot of pencils.

मेरे पास बहुत सारी पेंसिल हैं।

I have a lot of brushes and pencils.

मेरे पास बहुत सारे ब्रश और पेंसिल हैं।

Name

I Can...

- [ ] read the 1st sentence.
- [ ] read the 2nd sentence.
- [ ] make a sentence from a picture.
- [ ] color a picture.
- [ ] Draw a picture.

Santa is fat.

संता मोटा है।

Santa is having fun.

संता को मज़ा आ रहा है।

Name

I Can...

- [ ] read the 1st sentence.
- [ ] read the 2nd sentence.
- [ ] make a sentence from a picture.
- [ ] color a picture.
- [ ] Draw a picture.

I have one nose.

मेरी एक नाक है।

The one is saying its name.

एक अपना नाम कह रहा है।

Name

I Can...

- [ ] read the 1st sentence.
- [ ] read the 2nd sentence.
- [ ] make a sentence from a picture.
- [ ] color a picture.
- [ ] Draw a picture.

I have two ears.

मेरे दो कान हैं।

The number "two" is holding up bunny ears.

संख्या "दो" बनी कान पकड़ रही है।

Name

I Can...

- [ ] read the 1st sentence.
- [ ] read the 2nd sentence.
- [ ] make a sentence from a picture.
- [ ] color a picture.
- [ ] Draw a picture.

I have three buttons on my dress.

मेरी ड्रेस पर तीन बटन हैं।

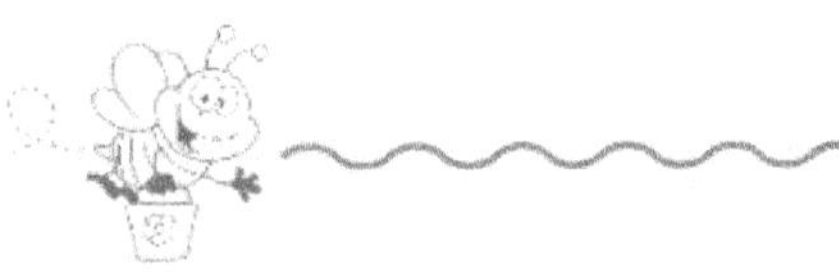

The number "three" is saying you got 3 out of 3.

संख्या "तीन" कह रही है कि आपको 3 में से 3 मिले।

Name

I Can...

- [ ] read the 1st sentence.
- [ ] read the 2nd sentence.
- [ ] make a sentence from a picture.
- [ ] color a picture.
- [ ] Draw a picture.

I have 0 tails.

मेरे पास 0 पूंछ हैं।

The number "zero" is saying, Ok.

संख्या "शून्य" कह रही है, ठीक है।

Name

I Can...

- [ ] read the 1st sentence.
- [ ] read the 2nd sentence.
- [ ] make a sentence from a picture.
- [ ] color a picture.
- [ ] Draw a picture.

I have five fingers on 1 of my hands.

मेरे 1 हाथ पर पांच उंगलियां हैं।

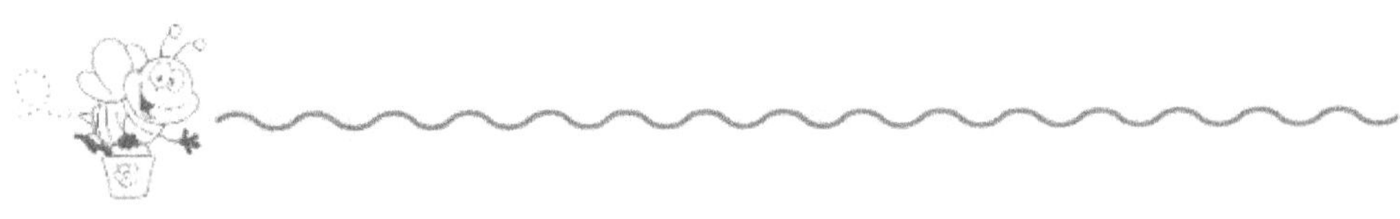

The number "five" is trying to give you a high five.

संख्या "पांच" आपको उच्च पांच देने की कोशिश कर रही है।

Name

I Can...

- read the 1st sentence.
- read the 2nd sentence.
- make a sentence from a picture.
- color a picture.
- Draw a picture.

My cat has four legs.

मेरी बिल्ली के चार पैर हैं।

The number "four" is counting to four.

संख्या "चार" चार की गिनती है।

Name

I Can...

- [ ] read the 1st sentence.
- [ ] read the 2nd sentence.
- [ ] make a sentence from a picture.
- [ ] color a picture.
- [ ] Draw a picture.

A butterfly has six legs.

एक तितली के छह पैर होते हैं।

The number "six" is saying 1+5=6.

संख्या "छह" 1 + 5 = 6 कह रही है।

Name

I Can...

- [ ] read the 1st sentence.
- [ ] read the 2nd sentence.
- [ ] make a sentence from a picture.
- [ ] color a picture.
- [ ] Draw a picture.

A spider has eight legs.

एक मकड़ी के आठ पैर होते हैं।

The happy and excited eight is holding up eight fingers

खुश और उत्साहित आठ अंगुलियों को पकड़े हुए है

Name 

I Can...

- [ ] read the 1st sentence.
- [ ] read the 2nd sentence.
- [ ] make a sentence from a picture.
- [ ] color a picture.
- [ ] Draw a picture.

The rooster is going to wake people up.

मुर्गा लोगों को जगाने वाला है।

The rooster is on the fence.

मुर्गा बाड़ पर है।

Name

I Can...

- [ ] read the 1st sentence.
- [ ] read the 2nd sentence.
- [ ] make a sentence from a picture.
- [ ] color a picture.
- [ ] Draw a picture.

My sister has nine stuffed animals.

मेरी बहन के पास नौ भरवां जानवर हैं।

The smiling number nine is saying its name out loud.

मुस्कुराता हुआ नौ जोर से अपना नाम कह रहा है।

Name

I Can...

- [ ] read the 1st sentence.
- [ ] read the 2nd sentence.
- [ ] make a sentence from a picture.
- [ ] color a picture.
- [ ] Draw a picture.

The baby bee has yellow and black stripes.

शिशु मधुमक्खी की पीली और काली धारियां होती हैं।

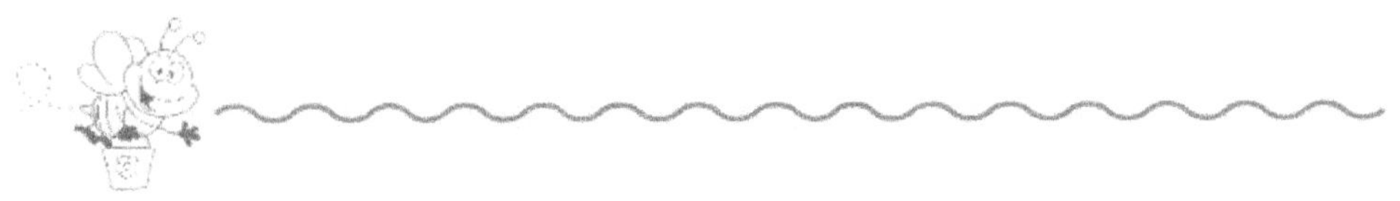

The bee is wearing a pink pacifier to calm itself.

मधुमक्खी खुद को शांत करने के लिए एक गुलाबी शांत करनेवाला पहनती है।

Name

I Can...

- read the 1st sentence.
- read the 2nd sentence.
- make a sentence from a picture.
- color a picture.
- Draw a picture.

The ladybug has many spots.

भिंडी में कई धब्बे होते हैं।

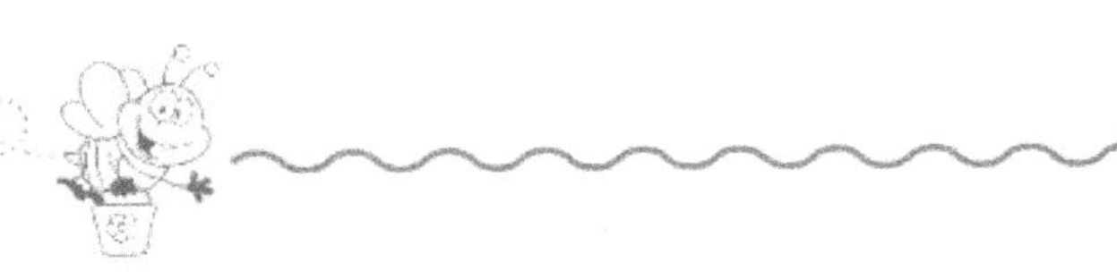

The red and black ladybug is just done eating some leaves.

लाल और काले रंग की भिंडी सिर्फ कुछ पत्तियां खाने के लिए बनाई गई है

Name

I Can...

- [ ] read the 1st sentence.
- [ ] read the 2nd sentence.
- [ ] make a sentence from a picture.
- [ ] color a picture.
- [ ] Draw a picture.

The sheep are skinny.

भेड़ें पतली होती हैं।

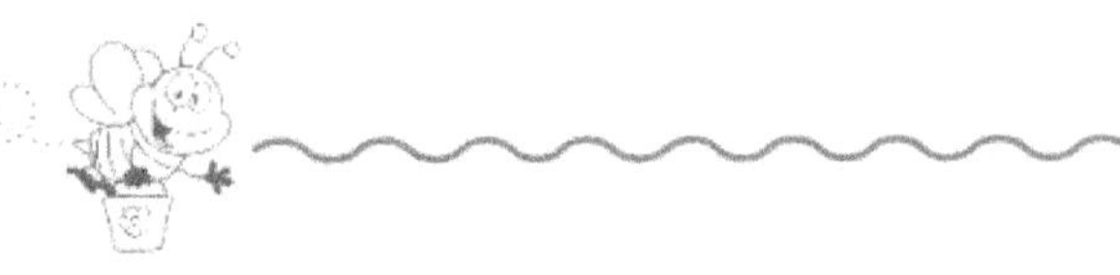

The white sheep have a lot of fluffy white wool to give away.

सफेद भेड़ों को दूर देने के लिए बहुत अधिक सफेद ऊन है।

Name

I Can...

- read the 1st sentence.
- read the 2nd sentence.
- make a sentence from a picture.
- color a picture.
- Draw a picture.

The rabbit is entering an egg painting contest.

खरगोश एक अंडा पेंटिंग प्रतियोगिता में प्रवेश कर रहा है।

The Easter Bunny is painting a chocolate egg.

ईस्टर बनी चॉकलेट चॉकलेट को चित्रित कर रही है।

Name

I Can...

- [ ] read the 1st sentence.
- [ ] read the 2nd sentence.
- [ ] make a sentence from a picture.
- [ ] color a picture.
- [ ] Draw a picture.

The owl is a language arts teacher.

उल्लू एक भाषा कला शिक्षक है।

An owl is teaching the kids in school about work.

एक उल्लू स्कूल में बच्चों को काम के बारे में पढ़ा रहा है।

Name

I Can...

- [ ] read the 1st sentence.
- [ ] read the 2nd sentence.
- [ ] make a sentence from a picture.
- [ ] color a picture.
- [ ] Draw a picture.

The man has an ancient hammer.

आदमी के पास एक प्राचीन हथौड़ा है।

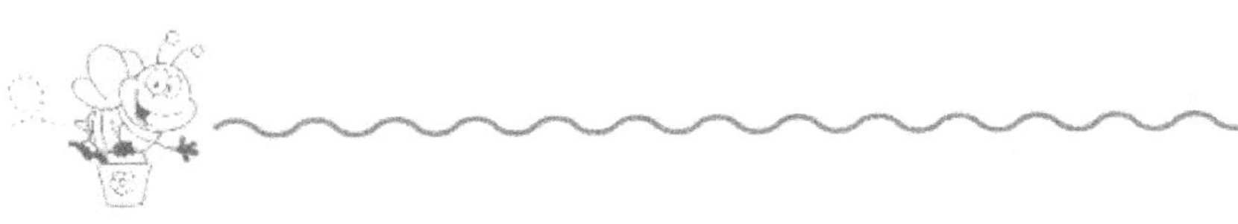

The builder man has gone to work on a project.

बिल्डर आदमी एक प्रोजेक्ट पर काम करने गया है।

Name

I Can...

- [ ] read the 1st sentence.
- [ ] read the 2nd sentence.
- [ ] make a sentence from a picture.
- [ ] color a picture.
- [ ] Draw a picture.

The goat has a friend.

बकरी का एक दोस्त है।

The old goat is proud of its golden bell.

पुरानी बकरी को अपनी सोने की घंटी पर गर्व है।

Name

I Can...

- read the 1st sentence.
- read the 2nd sentence.
- make a sentence from a picture.
- color a picture.
- Draw a picture.

My mom's friend is a maid.

मेरी माँ की सहेली एक नौकरानी है।

The maid is going to clean the hotel room.

नौकरानी होटल के कमरे को साफ करने जा रही है।

Name

I Can...

- read the 1st sentence.
- read the 2nd sentence.
- make a sentence from a picture.
- color a picture.
- Draw a picture.

I went to the zoo.

मैं चिड़ियाघर गया था।

The animals are having a big celebration.

जानवरों का बड़ा उत्सव हो रहा है।

Name

I Can...

- read the 1st sentence.
- read the 2nd sentence.
- make a sentence from a picture.
- color a picture.
- Draw a picture.

The dinosaur has a pillow.

डायनासोर का एक तकिया है।

The dragon is using the rock to build its house.

ड्रैगन अपने घर के निर्माण के लिए चट्टान का उपयोग कर रहा है।

Name

I Can...

- [ ] read the 1st sentence.
- [ ] read the 2nd sentence.
- [ ] make a sentence from a picture.
- [ ] color a picture.
- [ ] Draw a picture.

The boy is excited to go to school.

लड़का स्कूल जाने के लिए उत्साहित है।

The boy is late for school, so he is sprinting.

लड़का स्कूल के लिए देर हो चुकी है, इसलिए वह घूम रहा है।

Name

I Can...

- [ ] read the 1st sentence.
- [ ] read the 2nd sentence.
- [ ] make a sentence from a picture.
- [ ] color a picture.
- [ ] Draw a picture.

The kids on the school bus are going to school.

स्कूल बस में बच्चे स्कूल जा रहे हैं।

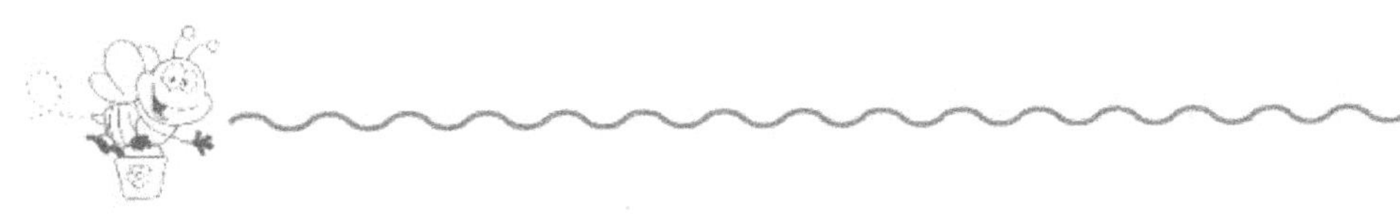

The children are going on a field trip on the yellow bus.

बच्चे पीली बस में फील्ड ट्रिप पर जा रहे हैं।

Name

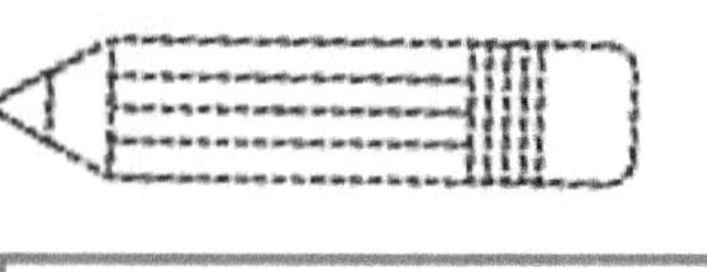

I Can...

- [ ] read the 1st sentence.
- [ ] read the 2nd sentence.
- [ ] make a sentence from a picture.
- [ ] color a picture.
- [ ] Draw a picture.

The cobra is very lovely.

कोबरा बहुत प्यारा है।

The rattlesnake is looking for its dinner.

रैटलस्नेक अपने डिनर की तलाश में है।

Name

I Can...

- [ ] read the 1st sentence.
- [ ] read the 2nd sentence.
- [ ] make a sentence from a picture.
- [ ] color a picture.
- [ ] Draw a picture.

That is a fat dog!

वह मोटा कुत्ता है।

This dog is wagging its tail for more treats.

यह कुत्ता अधिक व्यवहार के लिए अपनी पूंछ को हिला रहा है।

Name

I Can...

- [ ] read the 1st sentence.
- [ ] read the 2nd sentence.
- [ ] make a sentence from a picture.
- [ ] color a picture.
- [ ] Draw a picture.

The elephant lives in the zoo.

हाथी चिड़ियाघर में रहता है।

The elephant has a long trunk to spray water.

हाथी के पास पानी छिड़कने के लिए एक लंबा कुंड होता है।

Name

I Can...

- [ ] read the 1st sentence.
- [ ] read the 2nd sentence.
- [ ] make a sentence from a picture.
- [ ] color a picture.
- [ ] Draw a picture.

The giraffe eats vegetables.

जिराफ सब्जियां खाता है।

The giraffe has an extremely long neck.

जिराफ की गर्दन बहुत लंबी होती है।

Name

I Can...

- [ ] read the 1st sentence.
- [ ] read the 2nd sentence.
- [ ] make a sentence from a picture.
- [ ] color a picture.
- [ ] Draw a picture.

The chipmunk has a soft tummy.

चिपमंक में एक नरम पेट होता है।

The Chipmunk is about to eat a brown acorn.

चिपमंक एक भूरे रंग का बलूत खाने वाला है।

Name

I Can...

- [ ] read the 1st sentence.
- [ ] read the 2nd sentence.
- [ ] make a sentence from a picture.
- [ ] color a picture.
- [ ] Draw a picture.

I have ten toes in total.

मेरे कुल दस पैर हैं।

The one and the zero are holding hands.

एक और शून्य हाथ पकड़े हुए हैं।

Name

I Can...

- [ ] read the 1st sentence.
- [ ] read the 2nd sentence.
- [ ] make a sentence from a picture.
- [ ] color a picture.
- [ ] Draw a picture.

The alligator is jumping.

मगरमच्छ कूद रहा है।

The crocodile is excited.

मगरमच्छ उत्तेजित है।

Name ____________________ 

I Can...

- [ ] read the 1st sentence.
- [ ] read the 2nd sentence.
- [ ] make a sentence from a picture.
- [ ] color a picture.
- [ ] Draw a picture.

I found an ant.

मुझे एक चींटी मिली।

The ant is telling a story.

चींटी एक कहानी कह रही है।

Name

I Can...

- [ ] read the 1st sentence.
- [ ] read the 2nd sentence.
- [ ] make a sentence from a picture.
- [ ] color a picture.
- [ ] Draw a picture.

The bat sleeps upside down.

बल्ला उल्टा होकर सोता है।

The bat is ready to fly.

बल्ला उड़ने के लिए तैयार है।

Name ______________________

I Can...

- [ ] read the 1st sentence.
- [ ] read the 2nd sentence.
- [ ] make a sentence from a picture.
- [ ] color a picture.
- [ ] Draw a picture.

The cat is very tired.

बिल्ली बहुत थक गई है।

The cat is taking a nap.

बिल्ली झपकी ले रही है।

Name

I Can...

- [ ] read the 1st sentence.
- [ ] read the 2nd sentence.
- [ ] make a sentence from a picture.
- [ ] color a picture.
- [ ] Draw a picture.

The dog likes to play.

कुत्ते को खेलना पसंद है।

The dog is playing with a bone.

कुत्ता एक हड्डी से खेल रहा है।

Name

I Can...

- [ ] read the 1st sentence.
- [ ] read the 2nd sentence.
- [ ] make a sentence from a picture.
- [ ] color a picture.
- [ ] Draw a picture.

The elephant has eyelashes.

हाथी की पलकें होती हैं।

The elephant is shy.

हाथी शर्मीला है।

Name

I Can...

- read the 1st sentence.
- read the 2nd sentence.
- make a sentence from a picture.
- color a picture.
- Draw a picture.

The frog is hopping.

मेंढक हाँफ रहा है।

The frog is trying to catch the fly.

मेंढक मक्खी को पकड़ने की कोशिश कर रहा है।

Name

I Can...

- [ ] read the 1st sentence.
- [ ] read the 2nd sentence.
- [ ] make a sentence from a picture.
- [ ] color a picture.
- [ ] Draw a picture.

The goat is sleepily walking around.

बकरी सोते हुए घूम रही है।

The goat is eating grass.

बकरी घास खा रही है।

Name

I Can...

- read the 1st sentence.
- read the 2nd sentence.
- make a sentence from a picture.
- color a picture.
- Draw a picture.

The hippo has a big head.

हिप्पो का एक बड़ा सिर होता है।

The hippo has a big head.

हिप्पो का एक बड़ा सिर होता है।

Name

I Can...

- read the 1st sentence.
- read the 2nd sentence.
- make a sentence from a picture.
- color a picture.
- Draw a picture.

The iguana has a long tail.

इगुआना की एक लंबी पूंछ होती है।

The iguana is hiding behind the letter I.

इगुआना I के पीछे छिपा है।

Name

I Can...

- [ ] read the 1st sentence.
- [ ] read the 2nd sentence.
- [ ] make a sentence from a picture.
- [ ] color a picture.
- [ ] Draw a picture.

Mom bought a new bottle of jam.

माँ ने जाम की नई बोतल खरीदी।

There is jam on the bread.

रोटी पर जाम है।

Name

I Can...

- [ ] read the 1st sentence.
- [ ] read the 2nd sentence.
- [ ] make a sentence from a picture.
- [ ] color a picture.
- [ ] Draw a picture.

The kite has a beautiful tail.

पतंग की एक सुंदर पूंछ होती है।

The kite is on the ground.

पतंग जमीन पर है।

Name

I Can...

- [ ] read the 1st sentence.
- [ ] read the 2nd sentence.
- [ ] make a sentence from a picture.
- [ ] color a picture.
- [ ] Draw a picture.

The lion is timid.

शेर डरपोक है।

The lion is big.

सिंह बड़ा है।

Name

I Can...

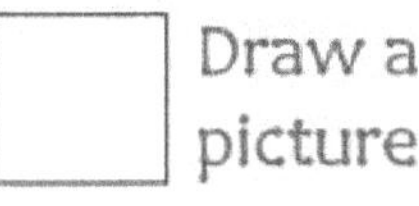

- [ ] read the 1st sentence.
- [ ] read the 2nd sentence.
- [ ] make a sentence from a picture.
- [ ] color a picture.
- [ ] Draw a picture.

I like mice.

मुझे चूहे पसंद हैं।

A rat is on top of the letter M

माउस M के ऊपर है

Name

I Can...

- [ ] read the 1st sentence.
- [ ] read the 2nd sentence.
- [ ] make a sentence from a picture.
- [ ] color a picture.
- [ ] Draw a picture.

The nose is breathing.

नाक से सांस चल रही है।

The letter N stands for a nose.

N एक नाक के लिए है।

Name

I Can...

- [ ] read the 1st sentence.
- [ ] read the 2nd sentence.
- [ ] make a sentence from a picture.
- [ ] color a picture.
- [ ] Draw a picture.

The octopus lives underwater.

ऑक्टोपस पानी के भीतर रहता है।

The octopus has eight tentacles.

ऑक्टोपस में आठ तम्बू होते हैं।

Name

I Can...

- [ ] read the 1st sentence.
- [ ] read the 2nd sentence.
- [ ] make a sentence from a picture.
- [ ] color a picture.
- [ ] Draw a picture.

The penguin eats fish.

पेंगुइन मछली खाता है।

The penguin lives in the arctic.

पेंगुइन आर्कटिक में रहता है।

Name

I Can...

- read the 1st sentence.
- read the 2nd sentence.
- make a sentence from a picture.
- color a picture.
- Draw a picture.

The queen has a wand.

रानी के पास एक छड़ी है।

The queen is beautiful.

रानी सुंदर है।

Name

I Can...

- [ ] read the 1st sentence.
- [ ] read the 2nd sentence.
- [ ] make a sentence from a picture.
- [ ] color a picture.
- [ ] Draw a picture.

The rabbit has long ears.

खरगोश के कान लंबे होते हैं।

The rabbit is thinking about something.

खरगोश कुछ सोच रहा है।

Name

I Can...

- [ ] read the 1st sentence.
- [ ] read the 2nd sentence.
- [ ] make a sentence from a picture.
- [ ] color a picture.
- [ ] Draw a picture.

The snake has polka dots.

सांप के पोल्का डॉट्स हैं।

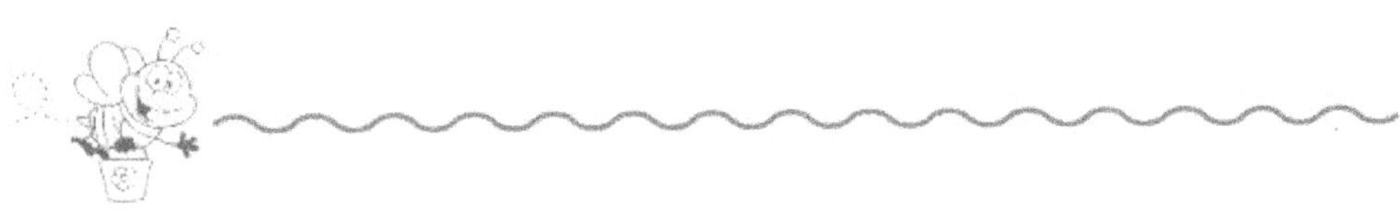

The snake is licking its lip because it is hungry.

सांप अपने होंठो को चाट रहा है क्योंकि उसे भूख लगी है।

Name

I Can...

- [ ] read the 1st sentence.
- [ ] read the 2nd sentence.
- [ ] make a sentence from a picture.
- [ ] color a picture.
- [ ] Draw a picture.

The tortoise has a pointy shell.

कछुए का नुकीला खोल होता है।

The turtle has a robust shell but is very slow.

कछुए के पास एक मजबूत खोल है लेकिन बहुत धीमा है।

Name

I Can...

- [ ] read the 1st sentence.
- [ ] read the 2nd sentence.
- [ ] make a sentence from a picture.
- [ ] color a picture.
- [ ] Draw a picture.

It's raining.

बारिश हो रही है।

We use the umbrella when it's raining.

बारिश होने पर हम छाता का इस्तेमाल करते हैं।

Name

I Can...

- read the 1st sentence.
- read the 2nd sentence.
- make a sentence from a picture.
- color a picture.
- Draw a picture.

The violin is a musical instrument.

वायलिन एक वाद्य यंत्र है।

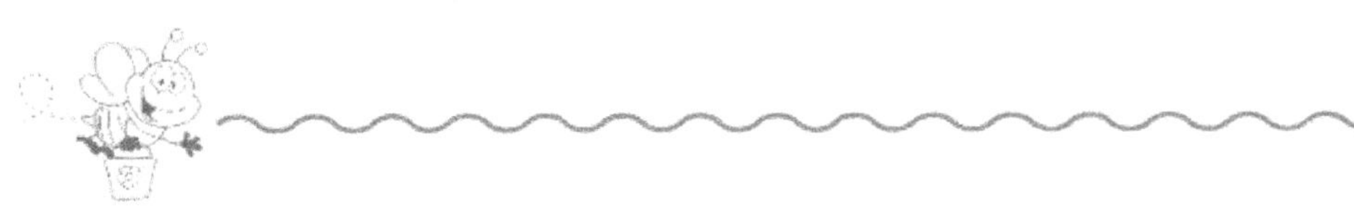

A violin can play beautiful music if played correctly.

यदि सही ढंग से बजाया जाए तो वायलिन सुंदर संगीत बजा सकता है।

Name

I Can...

- [ ] read the 1st sentence.
- [ ] read the 2nd sentence.
- [ ] make a sentence from a picture.
- [ ] color a picture.
- [ ] Draw a picture.

The walrus has a friend.

वालरस का एक दोस्त है।

The walrus has unusually sharp teeth.

वालरस में असामान्य रूप से तेज दांत होते हैं।

Name

I Can...

- [ ] read the 1st sentence.
- [ ] read the 2nd sentence.
- [ ] make a sentence from a picture.
- [ ] color a picture.
- [ ] Draw a picture.

The xylophone is a colorful instrument.

जाइलोफोन एक रंगीन यंत्र है।

The xylophone is an instrument like the piano.

ज़ाइलोफोन पियानो की तरह का एक उपकरण है।

Name

I Can...

- [ ] read the 1st sentence.
- [ ] read the 2nd sentence.
- [ ] make a sentence from a picture.
- [ ] color a picture.
- [ ] Draw a picture.

The boy has a little hat.

लड़के को थोड़ी टोपी है।

The boy is having fun playing with a yoyo.

लड़का एक योयो के साथ खेल कर मज़े ले रहा है।

Name

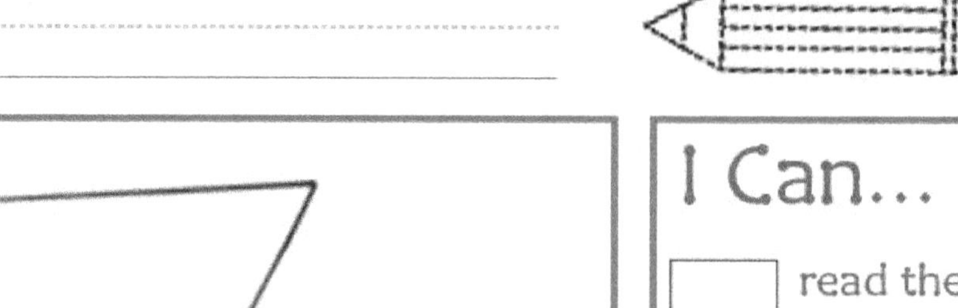

I Can...

- [ ] read the 1st sentence.
- [ ] read the 2nd sentence.
- [ ] make a sentence from a picture.
- [ ] color a picture.
- [ ] Draw a picture.

The zebra has a tail.

ज़ेबरा की एक पूंछ होती है।

The zebra has black and white stripes.

जेब्रा में काली और सफेद धारियां होती हैं।

Name

I Can...

- read the 1st sentence.
- read the 2nd sentence.
- make a sentence from a picture.
- color a picture.
- Draw a picture.

I have a candle on my cake.

मेरे केक पर एक मोमबत्ती है।

I had a small birthday cake for my party.

मेरी पार्टी के लिए मेरे पास एक छोटा सा जन्मदिन था।

Name

The astronaut is going on a mission.

अंतरिक्ष यात्री एक मिशन पर जा रहा है।

An astronaut has to explore our universe so that we would have more knowledge.

एक अंतरिक्ष यात्री को हमारे ब्रह्मांड का पता लगाना है ताकि हमें अधिक ज्ञान हो।

Name

I Can...

- [ ] read the 1st sentence.
- [ ] read the 2nd sentence.
- [ ] make a sentence from a picture.
- [ ] color a picture.
- [ ] Draw a picture.

The samurai is going for a morning jog.

समुराई सुबह की सैर के लिए जा रहा है।

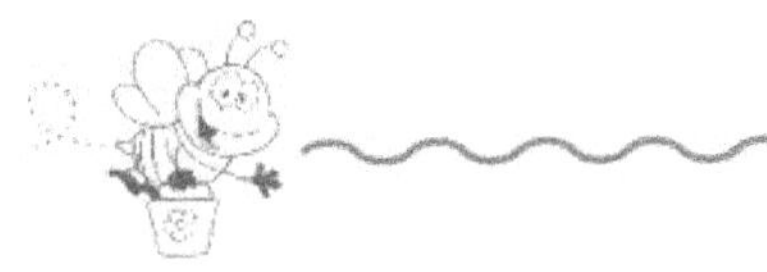

The samurai is training to become good at fighting.

समुराई लड़ने में अच्छा बनने का प्रशिक्षण ले रहा है।

Name

I Can...

- [ ] read the 1st sentence.
- [ ] read the 2nd sentence.
- [ ] make a sentence from a picture.
- [ ] color a picture.
- [ ] Draw a picture.

My friend is having a gigantic cake.

मेरे दोस्त एक विशाल केक है।

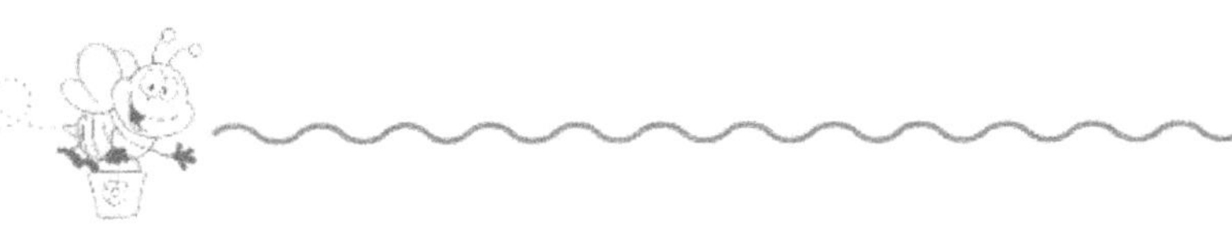

I had a humongous birthday cake for my celebration.

मेरे उत्सव के लिए मेरे पास एक विनम्र जन्मदिन का केक था।

Name

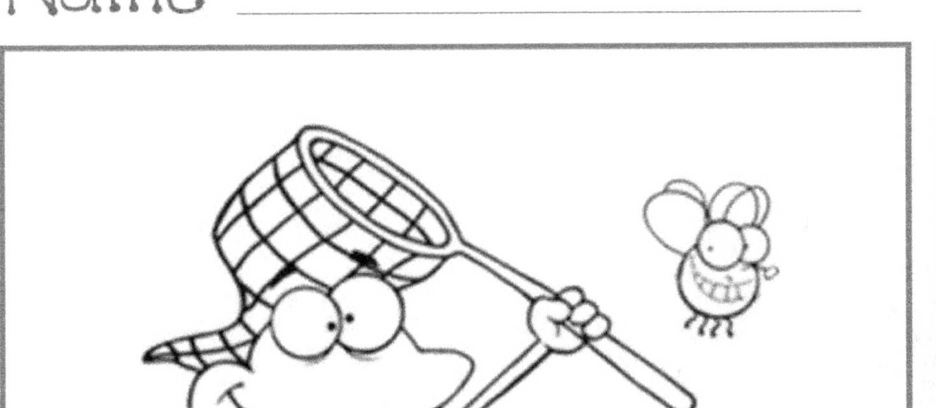

I Can...

- read the 1st sentence.
- read the 2nd sentence.
- make a sentence from a picture.
- color a picture.
- Draw a picture.

The frog is chasing the fly.

मेंढक मक्खी का पीछा कर रहा है।

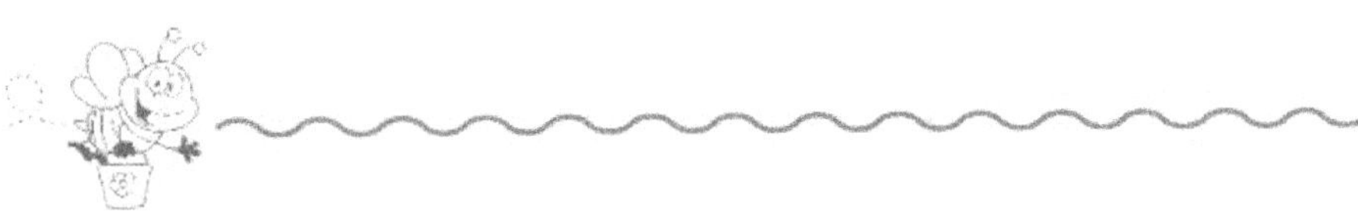

The green frog is trying to catch the fly.

हरा मेंढक मक्खी को पकड़ने की कोशिश कर रहा है।

Name

I Can...

- read the 1st sentence.
- read the 2nd sentence.
- make a sentence from a picture.
- color a picture.
- Draw a picture.

The ladybug has six legs.

भिंडी के छह पैर होते हैं।

The ladybug is on the leaf.

भिंडी पत्ती पर होती है।

Name

I Can...

- [ ] read the 1st sentence.
- [ ] read the 2nd sentence.
- [ ] make a sentence from a picture.
- [ ] color a picture.
- [ ] Draw a picture.

The dragon is sick.

अजगर बीमार है।

The dragon just ate something spicy, so he needed water.

ड्रैगन ने कुछ मसालेदार खाया, इसलिए उसे पानी की जरूरत थी।

Name

I Can...

- [ ] read the 1st sentence.
- [ ] read the 2nd sentence.
- [ ] make a sentence from a picture.
- [ ] color a picture.
- [ ] Draw a picture.

That is a baby cow.

वह एक शिशु गाय है।

A little cow is walking around near the barn.

थोड़ी सी गाय खलिहान के पास घूम रही है।

Name

I Can...

- [ ] read the 1st sentence.
- [ ] read the 2nd sentence.
- [ ] make a sentence from a picture.
- [ ] color a picture.
- [ ] Draw a picture.

The frog has a big smile.

मेंढक की बड़ी मुस्कान है।

The frog is smiling because it is happy.

मेंढक मुस्कुरा रहा है क्योंकि यह खुश है।

Name

I Can...

- read the 1st sentence.
- read the 2nd sentence.
- make a sentence from a picture.
- color a picture.
- Draw a picture.

The frog has a big mouth.

मेंढक का बड़ा मुंह है।

The frog is waving to us.

मेंढक हमारे पास लहरा रहा है।

www.ingramcontent.com/pod-product-compliance
Lightning Source LLC
LaVergne TN
LVHW080553160826
845677LV00010B/1826
* 9 7 9 8 6 5 2 7 5 9 2 5 4 *